D1455585

THE
BATHROOM
JOKE BOOK

by

Russ Edwards & Jack Kreismer

RED-LETTER PRESS, INC.
Saddle River, New Jersey

THE BATHROOM JOKE BOOK
Copyright ©2003 Red-Letter Press, Inc.
ISBN: 0-940462-38-9
All Rights Reserved
Printed in the United States of America

For information address:

Red-Letter Press, Inc.
P.O. Box 393, Saddle River, NJ 07458
www.Red-LetterPress.com

ACKNOWLEDGMENTS

Project Development Coordinator:
Kobus Reyneke

Cover design and typography:
s.w.artz, inc.

Editorial:
Jeff Kreismer

Significant Others:
Theresa Adragna
Kathy Hoyt, Robin Kreismer
Jim & Rory Tomlinson, Lori Walsh

INTRODUCTION

For more than twenty years, the original Bathroom Library has entertained people "on the go" everywhere.
With millions of copies out there, it proves that we're not all wet about bathroom reading.

Now, as heir to the throne, we proudly introduce a brand new Bathroom Library. We hope you enjoy this installment of it.

Yours flushingly,

Jack Kreismer
Publisher

**FOR AMERICA'S
FAVORITE READING ROOM**

THE
BATHROOM
JOKE BOOK

*Good, Clean Fun
for Comic Relief*

THE BATHROOM LIBRARY

RED-LETTER PRESS, INC.
Saddle River, New Jersey

A pair of elderly couples were chatting at dinner when one of the husbands said, "Bentley, how was that memory clinic you went to last week?"

"Great," answered Bentley. "We were taught all the latest and greatest memory helpers - association, visualization - that kind of stuff."

"Sounds good ... I might like to take a class. What was the name of it?"

Bentley's mind went blank. Then he suddenly smiled and said, "What do you call that flower that's red with a long stem and thorns?"

His buddy said, "You mean a rose?"

Bentley said, "Yeah, that's it," and then turned to his wife and and asked, "What was the name of that memory clinic, Rose?"

I once wanted to become an atheist, but I gave up — they have no holidays.
—Henny Youngman

> *You know what type of cosmetic surgery you never hear about? Nose enlargement.*
> —George Carlin

An itty-bitty turtle starts to climb a tree very slowly. After many hours, he finally reaches the top, jumps into the air frantically waving his front legs, and crashes into the ground, knocking himself silly. When he recovers, he slowly makes his way to the top of the tree again, jumps and falls just as hard to the ground. This happens time after time after time.

Two birds were sitting at the edge of a branch, watching painfully at what was happening. At one point, the female bird said to the male, "Honey, I think it's time to tell our little baby that he's adopted."

Stewardess: Would you like dinner?
Airline Passenger: What are my choices?
Stewardess: Yes or no.

A banker went fishing with one of his customers. They were out on a boat in the river when the vessel smashed into a rock and tipped over, spilling the guys into the drink. The customer noticed the banker flailing away and said, "Say, can you float alone?"

"Oh, c'mon!" exclaimed the banker. "I'm drowning and you want to talk business!?!"

I have a friend who's so into recycling she'll only marry a man who's been married before.

–Rita Rudner

> *You know you're getting old when you stoop to tie your shoes and wonder what else you can do while you're down there.*
>
> –George Burns

A woman comes home one day and says to her hubby, "Dear, the car won't start, but I know what the problem is. There's water in the carburetor."

The husband responds, "I don't mean to be disrespectful, but you wouldn't know the difference between a carburetor and a tailpipe."

The wife insists, "There's definitely water in the carburetor."

Finally, the husband says, "Okay, dear, I'll take a look at it. Where is it?"

"In the lake."

Two hillbillies are hunting when they come across some tracks in the woods.

"Look! Deer tracks," says the first hillbilly.

"Naah. Those are moose tracks. I know moose tracks when I see 'em," says the second hillbilly.

A few moments later they were run over by a train.

Q: **What did the navy captain say after he became a computer programmer?**

A: **"Don't give up the chip."**

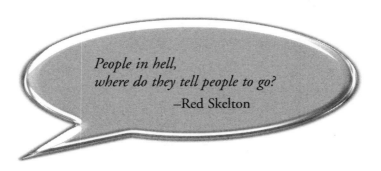

People in hell,
where do they tell people to go?
—Red Skelton

Ever notice how irons have a setting for "permanent" press? I don't get it.
            –Steven Wright

Did you hear about the two computers who got married and had a baby?

The first word it said was "Data."

Two rival politicos were together when one said, "I always relish the opportunity to promote my party. For example, whenever I'm at the airport I'll give the skycap a big tip and say, "Remember to vote Democratic."

His adversary responded, "I have my own way of doing just that - and it doesn't cost me a penny. I don't give any tip at all and I also say, 'Vote Democratic.'"

Three unemployed factory workers applied for a job at an ever-expanding food company. All three were hired by the big boss and subsequently interviewed by the foreman who expressed reservations about each of them. He said that one of the three had snapped for no apparent reason at his previous job. The second applicant had cracked up after severe stress ... And the third he believed was the father of the first two, who the foreman thought was a bit odd, though he couldn't put his finger on it.

The boss suggested keeping an eagle-eye on their work efforts. Reluctantly, the foreman agreed and asked in what food division they should be placed.

The head honcho replied, "It's a natural. Put them in our cereal area ... Snap, Crackle and Pop should be okay there."

If it wasn't for electricity, we'd all be watching television by candlelight.
—George Gobel

The other day I bought a wastebasket and carried it home in a paper bag. And when I got home, I put the paper bag in the wastebasket!

—Lily Tomlin

Two fellows are hunting in the

woods when one of them keels over and falls to the ground. The second guy panics. He calls 911 from his cell phone and says, "Help, help. I'm out here hunting with my friend and he suddenly dropped to the ground. I think he's dead."

The 911 operator responds, "Now, now. Calm down. First thing, you have to make sure he's dead."

BANG, BANG!

The hunter says, "Okay, he's dead. Now what do we do?"

Did you hear that because of U.S. Olympic gold medal skier Picabo Street's donations to a local Denver hospital, they're thinking about naming a new wing after her?

It's going to be called 'Picabo, I.C.U.'

Q: **What do you get when you cross a hospital with a skunk?**

A: **A medical scenter.**

A man walks into a doctor's

office with a banana in his left ear, a cucumber in his right ear and a carrot up his nose. He asks the doctor for his diagnosis and the doctor says, "You're not eating properly."

George Washington said to his father, "If I never tell a lie, how can I get to be president?"

—Red Buttons

Is sloppiness in speech caused by ignorance or apathy? I don't know and I don't care.

–William Safire

A husband and wife are awakened at two o'clock in the morning by a knock at the front door. The husband gets up and goes to the door where a stranger is asking for a push.

"No way," says the husband. "It's two in the morning!"

He closes the door and returns to bed.

His wife asks, "Who was that?"

"Just a stranger asking for a push."

"Did you give him one?"

The husband answers, "No, I didn't. It's two in the morning."

"Well you must have a short memory," says the wife. "Can't you recall about four months ago when our car broke down on our vacation. Two guys helped us then. Can't you help him now?"

The husband thinks better of it, goes to the front door and calls out into the dark,

"Hello - excuse me - are you still there?"

"Yes, I'm here."

"Do you still want a push?" asks the husband.

"Yes, yes, please!"

"Well, where are you?"

"I'm over here on the hammock."

Q: *What do you get when a Macintosh falls off a desk?*

A: *Apple turnover.*

I've been on so many blind dates I should get a free dog.

—Wendy Liebman

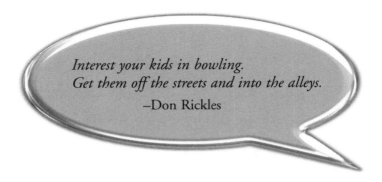

Interest your kids in bowling.
Get them off the streets and into the alleys.
—Don Rickles

You know of course that in Tibet, the Lama, as in Dali Lama, is spelled with one "l." The South American animal has a double "l" in its name but do you know what a three "l" lama is?

One heckuva big fire!

Two caterpillars are talking when, all of the sudden, a butterfly passes by. One caterpillar points upward and says to the other, "You'll never get me up in one of those things."

Ruppert Nerdock, the newspaper magnate, spent oodles of money to buy a racehorse. The noted trainer Willie Shumaker offered to race his horse against Nerdock's.

The night of the match race, the stands were filled and sportswriters from all of Nerdock's newspapers were there. Unfortunately for Nerdock, his horse didn't live up to its billing and was beaten by nine lengths. The next day, the sports page headline on all of Nerdock's newspapers read: NERDOCK'S HORSE FINISHES SECOND, SHUMAKER'S HORSE NEXT-TO-LAST.

Q: What do you get if you cross Bugs Bunny with computer software?

A: A rabbit with floppy ears.

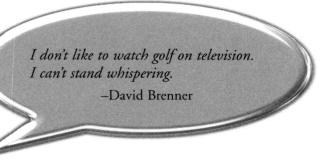

I don't like to watch golf on television. I can't stand whispering.

–David Brenner

> *It's amazing that the amount of news that happens in the world every day just exactly fits in the newspaper.*
>
> —Jerry Seinfeld

Patient: What's wrong, Doc? You look frustrated.

Doctor: I can't figure out just what the problem is. I think it may have to do with heavy drinking.

Patient: Okay, I'll just come back when you're sober.

Little Johnny was eating breakfast with his mother one morning when he innocently asked, "Mommy, how come Daddy doesn't have any hair on his head?"

"That's because he uses his head so much," answered his mother, proud that she came up with a quick response about her husband's baldness - or so she thought.

Johnny thought for a moment and then said, "So how come you have so *much* hair?"

A salesman applying for a position was asked about his professional background. He said, "I've had back-to-back jobs. The first was a hush-hush job at Sing Sing. Then, from time to time I was a door-to-door salesman with a fifty-fifty commission selling wall-to-wall carpeting day to day in Walla Walla."

"And would you say you were successful in both occupations?" asked the interviewer.

"So-so."

Q: **What did the ancient Romans yell on the golf course?**

A: **IV!**

Q: **Do you know the penalty for bigamy?**

A: **Two mothers-in-law.**

You know what I hate? Indian givers ... no, I take that back.

–Emo Phillips

> *My father invented the burglar alarm
> which, unfortunately, was stolen from him.*
> –Victor Borge

A guy is stopped for speeding.

The police officer makes his way to the driver's side of the car. The guy promptly rolls down his window and the cop says, "Let me see your driver's license."

The guy says, "I don't have a driver's license."

"Okay then, pop open your glove compartment and let's see your registration."

He says, "I don't have a registration. There's a gun in there."

The cop says, "A gun ... why's that in there?"

"I used it to shoot the woman I stole this car from."

"What!?! ... Where's the woman?"

"She's in the trunk."

At this point, the cop figures he'd better radio for backup. In no time, a squad of cars converge upon the vehicle. The police chief himself approaches the guy, still in the driver's seat, and says, "Let me see your driver's license."

The driver says, "Sure," and he produces his license.

Next, the chief asks for his registration. The driver reaches into the glove compartment and hands it to him at which point the chief asks, "Is there a gun in there?"

The driver answers, "See for yourself."

The chief walks around the car, looks in the glove compartment and sees that there's no gun. He then says, "Pop open your trunk."

The guy does so, the police chief looks in the trunk and there's no woman there. He walks back around to the driver's side and says, "What's going on here? One of my officers radioed for help because he said you had no driver's license, no registration, there was a gun in the glove compartment and a woman in the trunk."

The driver responds, "Yeah, and I bet he told you I was speeding, too."

> *One day my father took me aside and left me there.*
>
> —Jackie Vernon

I found out why cats drink out of the toilet. My mother told me it's because it's cold in there. And I'm like: "How did my mother know that?"

—Wendy Liebman

A couple of sour notes...

Q: What do you get when you drop a piano down a mine shaft?

A: A flat minor.

Q: What do you get when you drop a piano on an army base?

A: A flat major.

After seventeen years of analysis with his psychiatrist, Woody told his buddy," I always thought I was indecisive."

"And now?"

"I'm not so sure."

A Texan being tried on a murder rap in New York felt he wouldn't get a fair shake there so he bribed one of the jurors to find him guilty of a lesser charge, manslaughter. The jury was out for several days before they finally returned a manslaughter verdict. Afterwards, the Texan took the juror he bribed aside, thanked him and asked him how he managed to convince the others of the lesser crime.

"Well, it was pretty tough," said the juror. "The others wanted to acquit you."

Q: What do Eskimos get from sitting on the ice too long?
A: Polaroids.

I have no self-confidence. When girls tell me yes, I tell them to think it over.
—Rodney Dangerfield

People have been obsessed with fashion ever since the Garden of Eden, when Eve said to Adam, "You know, that fig leaf you have on is so last–season."

–Dennis Miller

It was a raw, rainy day in upstate New York but Mom, as usual, was bright and cheerful. As she went to wake up her son, he protested, "No, Ma, I don't want to go to school."

"But why not, son? Give me two good reasons why you don't want to get up."

"Well, for one, the kids hate me and, for another, the teachers hate me too."

"Oh, that's no reason not to go to school. Come on now - get ready."

"Give me two good reasons why I should go to school," the son demanded.

"Well, for one, you're 46 years old. And for another, you're the principal."

"Doc, I need help," said Ralph to his psychiatrist. "It may sound strange but I keep thinking that I'm a horse."

"I think I can cure you," the shrink answered, "but it's going to take some time and it's going to be extremely expensive."

"Money's not a problem, Doc. I just won the Kentucky Derby."

Maybe you've heard about the upcoming merger of UPS and Fed Ex?

They're going to call it Fed Up.

If all the nations in the world are in debt, where did the money go?
—Steven Wright

I'm not offended by all the dumb-blonde jokes, because I know I'm not dumb. And I also know that I'm not blonde.

—Dolly Parton

A soccer mom was delivering a mini-van full of little kids home one day when a fire truck zoomed past, sirens wailing and lights flashing.

Sitting prominently in the front seat of the fire truck was a Dalmatian dog.

That sparked a discussion of the dog's duties among the children.

"They use him to keep crowds back," said one youngster.

"No," said another, "he's just for good luck."

Then a a third child settled the argument once and for all when she said, "They use the dog to find the fire hydrant."

The other kids were always teasing little Johnny. They seemed to think that he was on the slow side. To prove it, every day they gathered a bunch of kids together in the schoolyard and called Johnny over.

"Hey, Johnny," taunted the ringleader. "I'm holding a dime in this hand and a nickel in this hand. Which one would you take?"

Without fail, day after day, Johnny took the nickel.

One day, a teacher heard word of the kids making fun of Johnny and called him in for a conference.

"Johnny, those children think you're not so bright. They don't think you know the difference between a nickel and a dime. I know you do, but can you tell me why you always take the nickel?"

"Well Mrs. Jones," Johnny answered, "If I took the dime, they wouldn't do it anymore."

The reason it's called "golf" is that all the other four-letter words were taken.
—Leslie Nielsen

My uncle's funeral cost us $5,000 so far. We buried him in a rented tuxedo.
–Dave Madden

BUMPER SNICKERS

HORSE LOVERS ARE STABLE PEOPLE.

WILL ROGERS NEVER MET A LAWYER.

HUMPTY DUMPTY WAS PUSHED.

WATCH MY BEHIND, NOT HERS.

HERE TODAY, GONE TO BORROW.

I BRAKE FOR TAILGATERS.

JESUS SAVES, I SPEND.

WATCH OUT! I DRIVE LIKE YOU DO.

THIS SPACE FOR RENT.

MY KARMA RAN OVER YOUR DOGMA.

Morris went to a psychiatrist.

"Doc," he said, "I'm going crazy. Every time I get into bed, I imagine there's somebody hiding under it."

"Just give me three years at three sessions a week and I'll have you cured," said the shrink.

"How much do you charge?" asked Morris.

"A hundred dollars per visit."

Morris thanked him and left.

Six months later the doctor ran into Morris on the street. "I remember you. You're the fellow who kept imagining someone under his bed. Why didn't you ever come in for treatment?" asked the psychiatrist.

"Because a bartender cured me for ten dollars."

"How'd he do that?"

"He advised me to saw the legs off the bed."

I went to a bookstore and I asked the woman behind the counter where the self-help section was. She said, "If I told you, that would defeat the whole purpose."

–Brian Kiley

It's time to go on a diet when the man from Prudential offers you group insurance. Or when you take a shower and have to let out the shower curtain. Or when you're standing next to your car and get a ticket for double parking.

—Totie Fields

A guy walks into a tavern and says to the bartender, "I'll have three shots, one for both of my best friends and one for me."

This goes on for a few weeks until, one day, he only orders two drinks. The bartender quizzically asks, "What happened, did one of your friends die?"

"No, I stopped drinking."

Q: *What do you get when you cross an elephant with a nymphoniac?*

A: *A half-ton pickup.*

Q: What's the difference between liberal arts graduates and government bonds?

A: Government bonds eventually mature and earn money.

A priest, a minister and a rabbi walk into a bar. The bartender takes one look at them and says, "What is this - some kind of a joke?"

A king was fanatical about hunting and spent virtually all of his time doing so. Finally, the people in his kingdom became fed up with his pastime and overthrew him. In all of history, this is the only known example of reign being cancelled on account of game.

I flew to London on the Concorde. It goes faster than the speed of sound, which is fun. But it's a rip-off because you couldn't hear the movie until two hours after you got there.

—Howie Mandel

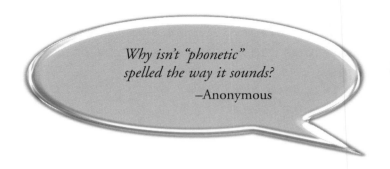

*Why isn't "phonetic"
spelled the way it sounds?*
—Anonymous

PONDERINGS FOR THE POTTY

Always remember you're unique ...
just like everyone else.

When Marcel Marceau dies,
will there be a moment of silence at his funeral?

Why are there interstate highways in Hawaii?

How come wrong numbers are never busy?

What happens if you get scared half to death twice?

How do you tell when you run out of invisible ink?

Did you ever wonder why we use caller I.D.
to screen calls and then have Call Waiting
so we won't miss a call from somebody
we didn't want to talk with in the first place?

A cannibal chief captured a man and asked him, "What is your job?"

The guy replied, I'm the editor of my company's newspaper."

"Ah," said the cannibal, "and soon you will be editor-in-chief."

Patient: Doc, I have some dimes stuck in my ear.

Doctor: How long have they been there?

Patient: About six months.

Doctor: Why didn't you come sooner?

Patient: I didn't need the money.

Trust your husband, adore your husband, and get as much as you can in your own name.

—Joan Rivers

> *What kind of crazy world is it when the only person we have to defend us is a lawyer?*
>
> —Merrit Malloy

One bitter winter night in Alaska, it was cold enough to neuter a brass monkey. Zeke was whooping it up at his favorite saloon when the bartender said to him, "Zeke, you owe quite a bit on your bar tab."

"Sorry," answered Zeke, "I'm flat broke this week."

"That's okay," said the bartender. "I'll just write your name with the amount you owe me right here on the wall."

"But," says Zeke, "I don't want any of my buddies to see that."

"No problem," said the bartender. "I'll just hang your parka over it until it's paid up."

A woman called a psychiatrist

and said, "Doc, you've got to help me! My husband thinks that he's in the opera. He sings all day at the top of his lungs and it's driving me nuts!"

"Calm down ma'am. Have him come see me tomorrow," the shrink said.

A couple of weeks later the wife called the psychiatrist.

"I don't know how you did it, but I've got to thank you. My husband's hardly singing anymore. Is he cured?"

The shrink responded, "Well, not exactly. I just gave him a much smaller part."

Did you hear about the popular shipboard improv show?

It's called "Cruise Line is it Anyway?"

The reason grandparents and grandchildren get along so well is that they have a common enemy.

—Sam Levenson

I was stopped once for going 53 in a 35 mph zone, but I told them I had dyslexia.

—Spanky McFarland

Bathroom Bits

Did you hear the one about the crooks who broke into the police station and stole all the toilet seats?

The cops have nothing to go on.

The only time the world beats a path to your door is if you're in the bathroom.

Q: How many men does it take to change a roll of toilet paper?

A: Nobody knows - it's never happened.

Three businessmen were on a deep sea fishing charter out of Hawaii and the first guy said, "I had a horrible fire. It destroyed everything. Now the insurance company is paying for everything so that's why I'm able to be here."

The second businessman said, "I had a terrible explosion which wiped out my building. The insurance company is paying for it so that's why I'm here, too."

The third businessman said, "What a coincidence. I had a terrible flood which destroyed everything. The insurance company is making good on it and that's why I could be here as well."

Confused, the other guys turned to him and said, "Flood? How do you start a flood?"

The trouble with unemployment is that the minute you wake up in the morning you're on the job.
            –Slappy White

Outside of a dog, a book is man's best friend. Inside of a dog, it's too dark to read.

–Groucho Marx

On a wild and windy Oregon beach, a woman found an ancient lamp. As soon as she picked it up a genie appeared.

"I am the genie of the lamp, yada-yada-yada. I'm sure you know how this goes, lady. What I have to tell you though is, that due to downsizing and cutbacks, you only get one wish - not three - so make it a good one."

"Well, goodness, that isn't difficult. I wish for peace in the Middle East."

"Peace in the Middle East?" the genie responded incredulously.

With that, the woman drew a rough map in the sand with a stick.

"I want these countries to stop fighting and live in peace with their neighbors."

"Hey, lady," explained the genie, "these people have been fighting for thousands of years. I'm good but not that good. You'll have to make another wish."

Thinking it over for a moment, the woman brightened and said, "Well, I've never been able to find Mr. Right. I want a man who isn't obsessed with sports, who can express emotion, who pays no attention to other women and who doesn't mind helping with the household chores."

The genie gave her a blank stare for a moment and then said, "Let me see that map again."

Then there was the dentist who complimented the hockey player on his nice, even teeth: one, three, five, seven and nine were missing.

The woman I've been seeing says she eats like a bird. Birds consume four times their weight in food every day. I'll be dating a round robin in no time.

–Scott Wood

> *Last night I dreamt I had insomnia. When I woke up, I was completely exhausted but too well rested to go back to sleep.*
> –Bob Nickman

A sheriff pulled a car over and found a panicked little old lady at the wheel.

"Ma'am, I couldn't help but notice that you were swerving all over back there," drawled the county mountie.

"Oh, officer - I almost had a horrible accident. I looked up and saw a tree right in front of me. I threw the wheel to the left and there was another tree in front of me. I threw the wheel to the right and there was another tree right in front of me."

The sheriff peeked into the car and checked out the rear view mirror.

"You can calm down now, Ma'am. That was your air freshener."

Guy: Will you marry me?

Girl: No.

And they lived happily ever after.

"Doctor, we've got an emergency! My baby just swallowed all my golf tees."

"I'll be there at once."

"What should I do till you get here, Doc?"

"Practice your putting."

Q: Why do they call it politics?

A: From the Latin, "poli," meaning many and "tics," meaning "bloodsucking parasites."

I got an A in philosophy because I proved my professor didn't exist.

—Judy Tenuta

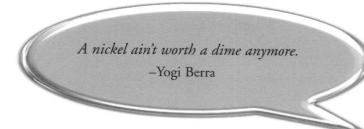

A nickel ain't worth a dime anymore.
–Yogi Berra

A New York lawyer was deer hunting in the backwoods of South Carolina. Making his way through the brush, he was stopped by a grizzled old backwoodsman.

"Hey you! Get out of here! This is private property."

"Listen," the lawyer replied. "You may think I'm a city slicker but I know my way around. This is public property and I can hunt here any time I so choose. I'm one of the top litigators in the country and if you give me any more trouble, I'll sue you and take everything you've got. I'll make so much trouble for you that you'll wish that you'd never been born."

"Well city boy, if'n you knew anything at all, you'd know that around here, we don't use courts and judges to settle arguments. We use the Carolina Three Kick Rule."

"What's that?" asked the attorney.

The old woodsman replied, "Well, first I kick you three times, then you kick me three times and we go on like that until somebody gives up."

The lawyer sized up the old man and figured he could take this guy easy.

"Okay, you're on," he said and with that the woodsman landed his thick boot where it would do the most damage. As the lawyer doubled over and slumped to the ground, he wondered how this old guy managed to kick like a mule.

"Here comes number two," the woodsman barked just as his boot smashed the lawyer in the teeth, knocking him off his knees and scattering his choppers all over the ground.

The woodsman's last kick came with no warning and impacted the lawyer's head so hard it spun him over and over until he came to rest in a briar patch. Severely injured and dazed, the arrogant lawyer struggled to his feet, thirsting for revenge.

"All right, bubba, you've had your fun," he snarled. "Now it's my turn."

The woodsman shrugged and replied, "Naw - you win. You can hunt here."

Never go to a doctor whose office plants have died.

—Erma Bombeck

Ninety-eight percent of the adults in this country are decent, hard-working, honest Americans. It's the other lousy two percent that get all the publicity. But then - we elected them.

—Lily Tomlin

Customer: Did you get my brakes fixed?

Mechanic: No, sorry I wasn't able to get them working but I took care of it anyway.

Customer: What'd you do?

Mechanic: I made your horn louder.

Rodney came home from his first day on the job at the sausage factory.

"How'd it go?" asked his wife.

"Terrible," Rodney answered. "I'm not going back."

"But why not?" asked his wife.

"Would you be willing to put up with sloppiness, poor workmanship, drinking on the job and foul language?"

"Absolutely not."

"Well neither would they."

Lawyer Q&A

Q: What do you call a lawyer who has really gone bad?

A: Senator.

Q: Do you know how copper wire was invented?

A: Two lawyers fighting over a penny.

Q: Have you heard about the new sushi bar that caters exclusively to lawyers?

A: It's called Sosumi.

Q: What's the difference between a trampoline and a lawyer?

A: You take your shoes off to jump on a trampoline.

To my wife double parking means on top of another car.

—Dave Barry

> *Well, enough about me. Let's talk about you. What do you think of me?*
> —Bette Middler

A minister, priest, and a rabbi get together weekly for a small stakes game of poker. The local police learn that they're doing some gambling and one night raid their game. They're taken to the hoosegow and appear before a judge in front of a packed courtroom the next morning.

The judge looks at the priest and says, "Father, I hear you've been doing some gambling. Is this true?"

The priest mutters to God to please forgive him for the white lie he's about to tell, then says, "Why, no ... of course not, your Honor."

The judge says, "Okay, you're free to go, Father," then turns to the minister and says, "Reverend, is it true that you've been gambling?"

The minister also asks forgiveness from God before saying, "No, I haven't been gambling, your honor."

The judge excuses the minister and asks the rabbi, "Have you been gambling?"

The rabbi answers, "With who?"

A tour guide was showing a vacationer around Washington, D.C. The guide pointed out the place where George Washington supposedly threw a silver dollar across the Potomac River.

"That's impossible," said the tourist. "No one could throw a coin that far!"

"You have to remember," answered the guide. "A dollar went a lot farther in those days."

Somebody said to me "But the Beatles were antimaterialistic." That is a huge myth. John (Lennon) and I literally used to sit down and say, "Now, let's write a swimming pool."

–Paul McCartney

> *I'm learning Spanish by calling my bank and pressing the #2 button.*
> —Paul Alexander

The Top Ten Ways To Enjoy Yourself at Other People's Expense

The authors of this book have carved the word "nudge" into an artform. Here, among their unlimited ways to annoy people, is their top ten.

#10　Sniffle incessantly.

　#9　Write the surprise ending to a novel on its first page.

　#8　Drum on every available surface.

　#7　At a golf outing, yell, "Swing-batabatabata-suhwing-batabata!"

　#6　Switch television channels five minutes before the end of every show.

　#5　Buy lots of orange traffic cones and reroute streets.

#4 Leave restaurant tips in Bolivian currency.

#3 At the laundromat, use one dryer for each of your socks.

#2 Pull over to the side of the road, roll down your window and point a hair dryer at cars to see if they slow down.

And the #1 reason to enjoy yourself at other people's expense- _____.

"Waiter, why isn't there any soup on the menu?"

"I wiped it off."

I went to a Halloween party dressed as the equator. As people walked toward me they got warmer.

—Steven Wright

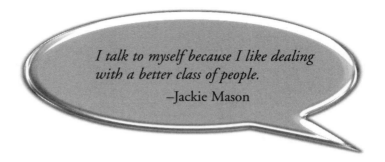

I talk to myself because I like dealing with a better class of people.
–Jackie Mason

An out of work actor got a job cleaning up the animal pens at the zoo. A fews days after he started, the zoo's star attraction, a 500 pound gorilla, died.

Frantic, the zoo director called the actor in and asked him if he'd be willing to put on a gorilla suit and impersonate the late, great ape.

Since it meant a big raise and a chance to be "top banana," the actor was happy to oblige and entertained the zoo's visitors with all sorts of hilarious shtick.

As the weeks went by, however, the visitors seemed to drift away to spend more and more time at the lion pit next door.

Trying to win back his following, the actor climbed a tree and shinnied out a long branch hanging over the lion's enclosure. He tormented the beast by throwing banana peels and screeching wildly. This delighted the audience and the gorilla was once again the star of the zoo.

One day, the tree branch cracked and fell into the lion's den along with the hapless gorilla impersonator.

The enraged lion attacked the actor who screamed, "Help me! Help me! I'm too young to die!"

The lion lowered his head right into the gorilla's mask and snarled, "Be quiet, you idiot. Do you want to get us both fired?"

"Lilly, will you marry me?" proposed the grandfather clock manufacturer.

"I'm afraid I can't, Bentley. My father told me to never hook up with a clockmaker."

"Why's that?"

"He said you'd always be working overtime."

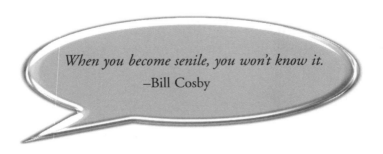

When you become senile, you won't know it.
—Bill Cosby

They should put expiration dates on clothes so we would know when they go out of style.
—Garry Shandling.

Q: Why was Cinderella a lousy football player?

A: Because she had a pumpkin for a coach.

A vacationer in Africa sees an old witch doctor lying in the road with his ear to the ground. He gets a little closer and hears the witch doctor mumbling, "Man in van, come by half an hour ago."

"Wow! You can tell that by listening to the ground?"

"No. He run over me."

Horace was at the airport waiting to

board the plane with plenty of time to spare. He went to the men's room where he noticed the latest and greatest, a computer that would give you not only your weight but would also tell you something about yourself. He inserted a quarter into the slot, and the computer screen displayed this message: "You're 185 pounds, you're looking for new business and that's why you're headed for Dallas."

Horace was dumbfounded, doubly-so when he saw another man step on the scale, pop in a quarter and the computer displayed, "You're 205 pounds and you're headed for a job interview in Boston."

Horace asked the man if this was true and he replied in the affirmative. Amazed, Horace changed his clothes in the stall of the men's room, took off his glasses and mussed up his hair to deceive his looks. He got back on the scale, inserted the obligatory change and the computer computer display read: "You still weigh 185, you're still looking to expand your business, and you just missed your flight to Dallas."

Never tell a woman that you didn't realize she was pregnant until you're certain that she is.

—Dave Barry

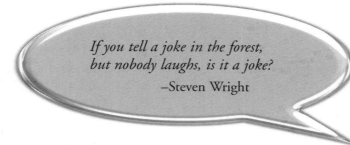

*If you tell a joke in the forest,
but nobody laughs, is it a joke?*
—Steven Wright

Three psychiatrists were at a local bar
and got more than a little tipsy toasting each other's
success.

The first psychiatrist said, "I have to admit
something - something I'd only ever tell you two.
I write prescriptions for drugs which I get kickbacks
for and don't report to the IRS."

The second psychiatrist said, "I have to confess
something too. As you know, I have a lot of celebrity
patients and whenever one makes a juicy revelation in
therapy, I sell the tip to the tabloids for big bucks."

After the two shrinks chuckle about they're
admissions, they turned to the third and asked him
what his deepest, darkest secret was.

"Well," the third psychiatrist said, "No matter how
hard I try, it seems I just can't keep a secret."

Q: What do you get if you divide the circumference of a pumpkin by its diameter?

A: Pumpkin pi.

Farnsworth: So are you going to hire that new secretary? I hear she's really gorgeous.

Brentwood: Yeah, but I don't know how smart she is.

Farnsworth: Oh? What do you mean?

Brentwood: Well, on her employment application where it says 'Sign here,' she put 'Pisces.'

Did you ever notice that when you blow into a dog's face he gets mad, but when you take him in a car he sticks his head out the window?

—Steve Bluestein

Never hire anybody whose resume rhymes.
–Anonymous

WISDOM FROM THE WALLS

EVER WONDER WHAT HAPPENED TO
PREPARATIONS A THROUGH G?

THE COST OF LIVING HASN'T AFFECTED ITS
POPULARITY.

IF I MELT DRY ICE,
CAN I TAKE A BATH WITHOUT GETTING WET?

IF VEGETARIANS EAT VEGETABLES,
WHAT DO HUMANITARIANS EAT?

BEFORE YOU GIVE SOMEBODY A PIECE OF YOUR
MIND, BE SURE YOU CAN SPARE IT.

EVER STOP TO THINK
AND THEN FORGET TO START AGAIN?

WHY DO WE WASH BATH TOWELS?
AREN'T WE CLEAN WHEN WE USE THEM?

Q: *What do you call a cow with no legs?*

A: *Ground beef.*

An elderly man was at home on his deathbed. He smelled the aroma of his favorite cookies baking. He craved for one last chocolate chip cookie before he died. He fell out of bed, crawled to the landing, then down the stairs and finally to the kitchen where his wife was baking.

With waning strength he made his way to the table and was just barely able to lift his arm to the cookie sheet. As he grasped a warm, moist cookie, his wife suddenly whacked his hand with a spatula.

"Why?" he meekly and weakly said, "did you do that?"

She replied, "Because they're for the funeral."

Have you ever wondered if illiterate people get the full effect of alphabet soup?
—John Mendoza

I got a traffic ticket the other day so I went to see a lawyer who charges by the minute. When I asked him the first question he said, "Wwwwwwellllllll Mmmmmisssssssssster Aaaaaaaaaarrrrrrrrnnnnnnnneeeeeette..."

–Nick Arnette

The warden visited three prisoners who were to be executed the follow morning. His final task, as far as the trio was concerned, was to ask them what they'd like for their final meal. And so he did.

"I'd like filet mignon," said Willie the Weasel.

"Pizza with the works," requested Louie the Squealer.

"And how about you, Benny?" asked the warden, notebook in hand.

"I'd like strawberries, nothing but strawberries," said Benny, smacking his lips.

"But strawberries are out of season," the warden pointed out.

"That's okay," Benny smiled. "I'll wait."

SIGNS OF THE TIMES

In a veterinarian's waiting room:
BACK IN 5 MINUTES. SIT! STAY!

In a podiatrist's window:
TIME WOUNDS ALL HEELS

On the door of a maternity ward:
PUSH! PUSH! PUSH!

Q: *What do you get when you cross the Atlantic Ocean with the Titanic?*

A: *Halfway!*

There's no present. There's only the immediate future and the recent past.
—George Carlin

> *Marriage is a wonderful institution. But who would want to live in an institution?*
>
> –H.L. Mencken

One evening, a policeman was staking out a tavern for possible driving-under-the-influence variations.

When the bar closed, he saw a fellow come stumbling out, stagger to his car and fumble with his keys before he got into the driver's seat. Finally he started the engine and took off only to find the cop waiting for him. The officer approached the driver, read him his rights and gave the guy a breathalyzer test. The results showed a reading of 0.0. The cop demanded to know how that could be.

The guy responded, "Tonight, I'm the designated decoy."

It's been fairly well publicized that Albert Einstein would never tell a German bartender his name - because every time he did he got a beer.

A grasshopper walks into a bar and the bartender says, "Hey, we have a drink named after you."

The grasshopper responds, "Wow! You have a drink called Danny?"

Q: What's the difference between a fly and a mosquito?

A: You can't zip a mosquito.

Did you hear the one about the elephant at the computer store?

He wanted a model with lots of memory but no mouse.

I love flying. I've been to almost as many places as my luggage.

—Bob Hope

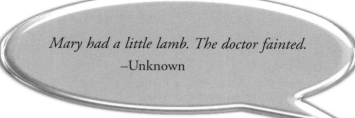

Mary had a little lamb. The doctor fainted.
—Unknown

And then there was the spider that had its own web site.

A small plane is flying with four people aboard: the pilot, a minister, a world-famous scientist and a drifter. The pilot announces that the plane is in deep trouble and they must flee for safety. "Unfortunately we only have three parachutes for the four of us," says the pilot.

The scientist exclaims, "I am the smartest man in the world. I must be saved." He grabs the parachute and jumps from the plane.

The minister volunteers, "I've lived a long time. The Lord awaits me. You two may take the remaining parachutes."

The drifter says, "Don't worry, Reverend. We've got one for you. The smartest man in the world just parachuted with my knapsack."

Q: *What do you get when you cross a comedic actress with a hockey player?*

A: *Goalie Hawn.*

A guy goes into a doctor's office with two bright red ears.

"Doc, this is really dumb. I was at the ironing board and the phone rang. Without thinking, I picked up the iron instead of the phone."

"Ouch! That's gotta hurt," said the doctor. "But what happened to the other ear?"

"Oh, that. They called back."

Happiness is having a large, loving, caring close-knit family in another city.

—George Burns

> *Be true to your teeth and they won't be false to you.*
>
> —Soupy Sales

A newly ranked second lieutenant walked into a military pool hall where two privates were engaged in a game of billiards. The officer asked the enlisted men if either of them had change for the soda machine. "Sure, buddy," one of the privates said as he pulled out a bunch of coins from his pocket.

"Ahem ... I think you may have a slight disregard for military protocol. Let's try this one more time, and this time salute and address me as 'sir.'"

The private gave the lieutenant a snappy salute and said, "No, sir, I don't have any change."

Q: Why is consumer advocate Ralph Nader humorless?

A: Because you can't recall a joke.

Two bees were having a conversation. One asked the other how things were going.

"Not very well," said the second bee. "The weather's been so wet that there are no flowers or pollen so I can't make honey."

"I've got some good news for you," said the other bee. "There's a Bar Mitzvah going on a few blocks down the road. You'll find loads of fruit and flowers there."

"Hey, thanks for the tip," the second bee said as it flew away.

A couple of hours later, the bees ran into each other again and the first bee asked, "How'd you make out?"

"Great. Thanks again for the advice."

"Uhh, I'm glad to oblige, but what's that thing doing on your head?" asked the first bee.

"Oh, that's my yarmulke," said the second bee. "I wanted to make sure they didn't think I was a wasp."

I had a boring job. I cleaned the windows in envelopes.

—Rita Rudner

Smartness runs in my family. When I went to school I was so smart my teacher was in my class for five years.

—Gracie Allen

Q: What happens if you don't pay your exorcist promptly?

A: You get repossessed.

Q: What do you get when you toss a hand grenade into a kitchen in France?

A: Linoleum blownapart.

"Why are you so late?" growled the boss.

"Well, boss ... the alarm clock woke up everybody but me this morning."

"Whaddaya mean by that?"

"There are seven people in our family and the alarm was set for six."

FOOD FOR THOUGHT

What's a cannibal's favorite kind of television show?
A celebrity roast.

And then there was the cannibal who ate his mother-in-law. She still disagreed with him.

Two cannibals were eating a comedian when one said to the other, "Does this taste funny to you?"

A couple of cannibals were at the dinner table when one said, "You know, I really don't like my mother-in-law." "Then just eat the vegetables."

When do cannibals leave the dinner table -
after everyone's eaten?

Two cannibals sat licking their fingers after a particularly large feast.
"Your wife makes a delicious roast," said one to the other.
"Thanks," the other said. "I'm going to miss her."

Two cannibal women are talking. One says, "I don't know what to make of my husband."
The other one says, "Get a recipe book."

Did you hear about the cannibals who captured a group of politicians? They had to buy a crock pot to cook them.

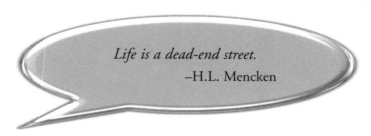

Life is a dead-end street.
–H.L. Mencken

People are going on dates now to coffee bars. This is the worst idea. Four cappuccinos later, your date doesn't look any better.

—Margot Black

It was Spring Break in Florida and

thousands of college kids overran the normally quiet town, raising a ruckus and turning it on its ear.

A student in baggy cut-offs and an Hawaiian shirt sauntered into the local bar asking for a beer. The bartender pointed to a sign that said patrons must wear a tie to be served.

Well, the young man had a real hankering for a cool one so he went out to his car to search for anything that resembled a tie. Not able to find anything else, he decided to wrap a pair of jumper cables around his neck. When he returned to the tavern, the barkeep said, "That's not a tie!"

"Sure it is. It's the latest fashion," insisted the lad.

"Well, okay," grumbled the bartender as he poured the brew. "Just don't start anything."

A traffic cop pulled over a car driven by a nun and said, "Sister, this is a 65 mile an hour highway. You're going too slow."

The puzzled nun replied, "But I just saw a sign that said 31."

"I understand now. You have it mixed up. That's the route number, not the speed limit sign," explained the officer. "One more thing before you go, Sister. Why are there two nuns hiding on the floor in the back seat?"

"Oh, I just turned off route 125."

The answer is deduce.
And the question?
What is the lowest card in de deck?

> *I was arrested today for scalping low numbers at the deli.*
> —Richard Lewis

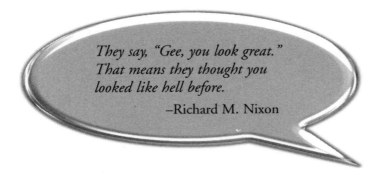

They say, "Gee, you look great."
That means they thought you
looked like hell before.

–Richard M. Nixon

On his first day of school, little

Johnny raised his hand to be excused to go to the bathroom.

A couple of minutes later he returned and said, "I can't find it."

The teacher drew him a little floor plan of the school and sent him out once again.

A few minutes later he returned and said, "I can't find it."

This time the teacher asked a boy from the second grade to take Johnny to the bathroom.

Shortly thereafter they came back and the teacher asked the older boy if little Johnny had any trouble finding it this time.

"Not at all, teach," replied the older boy. "He just had his underpants on backwards."

The head of the sales department

winced as his new assistant gave a report to the Board of Directors.

"This has been a really cool job. I was afraid that it was going to be lousy but it turned out really cool. The last time I did something like this it was lousy but the people here are cool so I was surprised at how cool it turned out when it could have been totally lousy."

After the meeting, the sales manager took his young assistant aside and said, "George, there are two words I don't want to hear you use in the future. One is cool and the other one is lousy."

"Fine," replied George. "So what are the two words?"

Gal: If we get engaged, would you give me a ring?

Guy: Sure – what's your number?

Earth Day was held recently. In honor of the event, I decided that I am just going to use only recycled jokes.

—David Letterman

Croutons are kept in a "stay-fresh" pouch. Croutons are stale bread. If we left these open all night they could only get better. Nobody has ever gone back to the store and said, "I need my money back. These are going fresh."

—Steve Bruner

A country hick made a trip to the big city and went on a shopping binge. Among other items, he bought a 24-piece jigsaw puzzle. When he got back home, he worked on it every night for a week when it was finally finished.

Proudly he showed it to his neighbor who said, "That's somethin', Clem. How long did it take you?"

Clem said, "Only a week."

His neighbor questioned, "I've never done a puzzle. Is that fast?"

"You bet," said Clem. "Why look right here at the box. It says 'from two to four years'."

Q: *What do you get when you cross a rabbit with a kilt?*

A: *Hopscotch.*

Once upon a time there was a lonely frog who called a telephone psychic service.

"You are going to meet a beautiful young woman who is very interested in you. She'll want to know all about you," said the psychic.

"Where am I going to meet this beautiful young woman - at a party?" croaked the frog.

"No," replied the psychic. "In biology class."

A guy comes home and finds his wife, a noted psychic, standing at the front door with a baseball bat in hand.

"You no good louse," she growled, "and just where were you until 3 A.M. tomorrow morning?"

Did you ever try to tell somebody they've got a little bit of dirt on their face? You can never get them to rub the right spot, can you?

–George Carlin

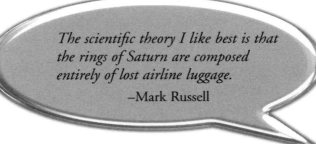

The scientific theory I like best is that the rings of Saturn are composed entirely of lost airline luggage.
—Mark Russell

SPORTS SHORTS

Why is it difficult to drive a golf ball?
Because it doesn't have a steering wheel.

What do old bowling balls become?
Marbles for elephants..

Why was the artist in the boxing ring?
Because the fight ended in a draw.

Why was Japanese ice hockey a failure at the box office?
No one had a yen for it.

What do you get if you cross a bowling lane with a famous heavyweight boxer?
Muhammad Alley.

Where did they put the matador who joined the baseball club?
In the bullpen.

Three elderly women were discussing the problems of aging.

The first one said, "You know, sometimes I'll be standing by the refrigerator with a bottle of milk and I can't remember whether I need to put it away or to use it for something."

The second said, "I know how it is. Sometimes I'm at the foot of the staircase and can't remember whether I was on my way up or on my down."

The third little old lady said, "Well, I'm glad I don't have that problem - knock on wood," as she tapped her knuckles against the table and then said, "Let's see ... Was that the front door or the back door?"

I've developed a new philosophy ...
I only dread one day at a time.
—Charlie Brown

It's no longer a question of staying healthy. It's a question of finding a sickness you like.

–Jackie Mason

Outside the main entrance to a

shopping mall, a man stood with a dog on a leash. The sign beside him said 'Talking Dog For Sale - $5.'

An incredulous vet stopped and said, "Sir, I have treated thousands of dogs in my 20 years of practice and I have yet to meet one who talks."

"Well you have now, buddy," piped up the pooch. "Not only do I talk, but I'm also the fastest dog in the world ... the fleetest greyhound eats my dust. I have a Masters Degree in math from Stanford, I'm a skilled pediatric surgeon, a world class surfer and I also hold 18 patents in genetic engineering."

"That's incredible!" stammered the flabbergasted vet to the owner. "Why on earth would you sell such a dog for only five dollars?"

"Because," the man replied, "I'm sick and tired of all his bragging."

Q: Where do they imprison the man who was convicted of assault and battery?

A: In a dry cell.

A New Yorker calls his mother who lives in Florida. She answers the phone with a very weak-sounding voice.

"Mom, you don't sound good. What's wrong?"

Very feebly she answers, "I haven't eaten in quite some time."

"How long has it been Mom?"

"My last meal was 26 days ago."

"26 days! How come?"

"I didn't want to be caught with food in my mouth when you called."

Anyone who says he can see through women is missing a lot.

—Groucho Marx

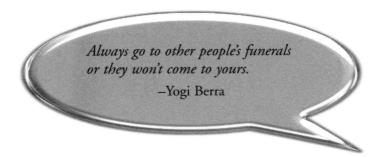

Always go to other people's funerals or they won't come to yours.
—Yogi Berra

A guy goes for a job at the CIA.

The interviewer says, "So you want to be an agent?"

He replies, "I'd do anything to work for the CIA."

The CIA representative then hands him a revolver and says, "Alright, I want you to go in the next room and shoot your wife."

The applicant hems and haws and says, "I can't do that. That's my partner for the rest of my life. I guess I'll have to pass on the CIA job."

A second man comes in for an interview. After a few questions, the CIA representative hands him a gun, too, and says, "If you really want to become an agent, go in the next room and shoot your wife."

The man responds, "No way. She's the love of my life and the mother of my three children."

A third applicant is given the same instructions, walks into the next room and closes the door. Gunshots ring out followed by the sounds of tables being overturned, lamps crashing and furniture being thrown around. Finally, the applicant emerges from the room and the interviewer says, "What happened in there?"

The wannabe agent replies, "The gun had blanks in it. I had to strangle her."

The hysterical woman charged into the police station screaming that her car had been stolen.

"Calm down, ma'am," advised the desk sergeant. "Do you have a description of the suspect?"

"No," the woman replied, fighting back tears, "but I did manage to get the license plate number."

My kid is mean. He tapes worms to the sidewalk and watches the birds get hernias.
—Rodney Dangerfield

I went into a general store. They wouldn't let me buy anything specifically.

–Steven Wright

In The Garden of Eden

Q: Why did God create Adam before Eve?

A: Because every great artist makes a rough draft before creating the masterpiece.

Q: Why did God create Adam before Eve?

A: So he wouldn't be bothered with suggestions.

Q: What did Adam say to Eve when she asked him if he loved her?

A: "Who else?"

Q: When was Adam born?

A: A little before Eve.

Q: Why did Eve move to New York?

A: She fell for the Big Apple.

When the Lord told Adam that he could provide him with a companion, one that would be his 'everything-you'd-want-a-woman-to-be,' Adam replied, "Gee, that's great."

"Just one thing," said God, "it's going to cost you an arm and a leg."

Adam responded, "What can I get for a rib?"

A fellow who was all out of birthday gift ideas for his mother-in-law wound up buying her a large plot in an expensive cemetery. For her next birthday, he bought nothing.

When she complained vociferously about his thoughtlessness he said, "Well, you didn't use the gift I gave you last year."

Only one man in a thousand is a leader of men — the other 999 follow women.

–Groucho Marx

> *Why is there always a mailbox in front of the post office?*
>
> –Gallagher

Q: What's the difference between congressmen and ex-cons?

A: Every so often, ex-cons pass a few good bills.

Two city workers were making their way down the street with one digging holes and the other filling them right back in.

A shopkeeper watched them for a bit, and being a dutiful taxpayer, he felt he had to confront them about what they were doing.

"I understand your concern," said one of the workers, "but it's really simple. We work as a threesome and the guy who plants the trees is sick today."

Q: *How do crazy people go through the forest?*

A: *They take the psychopath.*

Three old geezers were sitting on a city park bench. The one in the middle was reading a newspaper while the other two were pretending to fish. A policeman on the beat watched them as they baited imaginary hooks, cast their lines and reeled in their fake catches.

"Do you know these two?" the cop asked the guy reading the paper.

"Sure. They're buddies of mine."

"Well, their disturbin' the other people. You better get them outta here!"

"Yes, officer," said the guy, and with that he put down his newspaper and furiously began rowing.

I like a women with a head on her shoulders. I hate necks.

—Steve Martin

> *The reason there are two senators for each state is so that one can be the designated driver.*
>
> –Jay Leno

Stella lived the good life in Beverly

Hills. Married to a successful producer, she had everything a woman could want.

One evening, during one of her many fabulous parties, Stella passed out and was rushed to the hospital.

While on the gurney, she had a near-death experience. She saw God and asked, "Is my time over?"

God replied, "Not at all, Stella. You will live healthy and happy to a ripe old age."

Waking up in the recovery room, Stella vowed that if she had so many good years left she was going to make the most of it. She summoned a plastic surgeon and told him that she wanted to be scheduled for liposuction, a tummy tuck, a nose job, and a face lift. She also called in a beautician who dyed her hair and did her nails.

Stella was very pleased with her wonderful new self

and looked forward to getting on with her life, but as she left the hospital, she was run over by an ambulance and killed.

In another meeting with God, this time at the gates of Heaven, Stella complained, "I thought you said I'd live to a ripe old age."

God replied with surprise, "Stella? I'm sorry. I didn't recognize you."

A boxer's taking a licking and after round one he goes back to the corner where his trainer advises him, "When you get knocked down, stay down until eight."

The fighter says, "Okay … what time is it now?"

As a child my family's menu consisted of two choices: take it or leave it.

–Buddy Hackett

> *Early to rise and early to bed, makes a male healthy, wealthy and dead.*
>
> —James Thurber

A parrot, a parakeet and a mynah bird go into a bar. They order three beers. The bartender comes back with two beers, one for the parrot and one for the parakeet.

The mynah bird complains, "Hey, where's my beer?"

The bartender says, "Sorry, we don't serve mynahs here."

Boss: Well, you seem to have everything a job applicant should have ... and you've just gotten out of Yale. Now, what was your name again?

Job Applicant: Yohnson.

Q: What do you say to praise a computer?

A: "Data boy!"

Q: What part of the fish do most anglers bring home?

A: The tale.

A snail bought a particularly impressive race car and decided to enter the Indianapolis 500. To give the car a distinctive look, the snail had a big letter S painted on the hood, sides and trunk before the big race. When the race began, the snail's car immediately took the lead, prompting one of the spectators to say, "Look at that S car go!"

> I've always wanted to go to Switzerland to see what the army does with those wee red knives.
>
> –Billy Connolly

I think of my boss as a father figure.
That really irritates her.

—Mary Jo Crowley

A husband was troubled that his wife was experiencing some hearing loss so he sought the advice of a physician.

The doctor suggested a simple test to determine if, indeed, there was a problem.

When the fellow returned home that evening, his wife was preparing dinner at the stove.

"Hi, dear," he said in a normal tone of voice. "What's for dinner?"

No answer.

He took a few steps closer to his bride, as the doctor had suggested for this test, and then repeated, "What's for dinner?"

Still no response.

Then he moved directly behind her and shouted, "What's for dinner?"

His wife spun around and loudly exclaimed, "For the third time - pot roast! What are you, deaf!?!"

Sergeant First Class Ryan was assigned

to the induction center, where he advised new recruits about their rights and their benefits, particularly their GI insurance.

As time passed, Ryan's boss, Colonel Korn, noticed that the sergeant had close to a 100% record for insurance sales.

One day, rather than approach the sergeant, Colonel Korn decided to stand in the back of the room and hear Ryan's sales pitch to the new inductees.

Ryan explained the basics of the GI Insurance progam and then followed with: "If you have GI insurance and go into battle and are killed, the government has to pay $1 million to your beneficiaries. If you don't have GI insurance and you go into battle and are killed, Uncle Sam only has to pay $10,000."

"Now," he concluded, "You tell me which bunch are going to be sent into battle first?"

Sincerity is everything. If you can fake that, you've got it made.

—George Burns

There's no such thing as fun for the whole family; there are no massage parlors with ice cream and free jewelry.

—Jerry Seinfeld

They've just invented a microwave television. Now you can watch a three hour baseball game in four minutes.

When a salesman marries a saleswoman do they become sell-mates?

Grandma Gertrude reported to the doctor that she hadn't been able to go to the bathroom for almost two weeks despite sitting there for seemingly hours on end.

"Have you taken anything?" queried the MD.

"Oh, yes," replied Gertrude. "A book."

A hot dog vendor was at his usual place of business in New York's Central Park when a man came by, plucked down a one-dollar bill and walked away. The next day, the same thing happened - the man dropped a dollar bill on the counter and left. This went on for a couple of months until one day when the man left his customary currency, the vendor shouted after him.

The vendor shouted, "Wait a second, sir!"

The man said, "I figured at some point you'd ask why I hadn't taken a hot dog."

The vendor replied, "No ... I just want you to know that hot dogs are now $1.25."

Q: How many lawyers does it take to screw in a light bulb?

A: How many can you afford?

In China, do you think they call their good dishes America?
    —Wendy Liebman

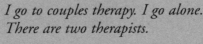

I go to couples therapy. I go alone.
There are two therapists.

—Garry Shandling

A magician working on a cruise ship had the
luxury of doing the same tricks over and over again
because the audience was always different - but there
was just one problem. The captain's parrot saw the
performances every week and began to understand all of
the illusions. Once he did, the bird began interrupting
the magician's shows by shouting out things like:

"Look, it's not the same hat!"

"Hey, why are all the cards the Ace of Spades?"

"Look, he's hiding flowers under the table."

The "Copperfield of the Cruise Liner" became
outraged but couldn't do anything about it since it was
the captain's parrot.

Then, one day, the ship had an accident and sunk. The
magician found himself lodged on a piece of wood in
the middle of the ocean. Of course, as fate would have
it, the parrot was right by his side. With an "if looks
could kill," they stared at each other for some time.

Finally, after a week or so, the parrot said, "Okay, I
give up. What did you do with the boat?"

A neutron walks into a bar and asks the bartender, "How much for a beer?"

The bartender looks at him and says, "For you, no charge."

A guy ran into a bar, ordered twelve shots lined up and started knocking them back as fast as he could.

The bartender asked, "Say pal, why are you drinking so fast?"

The guy replied, "You would too if you had what I have."

The bartender looked at him curiously and said, "What do you have, anyway?"

Drinking down the last shot, the guy answered, "An empty wallet."

I hate it when my foot falls asleep during the day because that means it's going to be up all night.

—Steven Wright

The reason lightning doesn't strike twice in the same place is that the same place isn't there the second time.

–Willie Tyler

A duck walks into a convenience store and asks, "Do you sell any grapes here?"

The manager says, "No, we don't sell grapes."

The next day the duck waddles into the store and asks, "Do you sell grapes here?"

The manager says, "No, we don't."

The third day the duck meanders into the store and asks, "Do you sell grapes here?"

The manager says, "Look! If I told you once, I told you three times, we don't sell any grapes here! The next time you come in here asking for grapes, I'm gonna nail your webbed feet to the wall!"

The next day the duck enters the store and asks, "Do you have any nails?

The manager says, "No. we don't sell nails here."

The duck says, "Good. Do you have any grapes?"

A guy prays to the Lord to win the lottery, promising to do good deeds when he gets lucky. This goes on for weeks, but the guy never wins. Finally, he says, "God, I dont understand. I'm a good person. I've been praying for a long time to win the lottery. How come I haven't?"

A thundering voice from the heaven responds, "You gotta buy a ticket!"

Q: *If two wrongs don't make a right, what do two rights make?*
A: *An airplane.*

Did you hear the one about the lawyer who frequented only posh restaurants? He was an ambiance chaser.

—Emo Phillips

Hospitals are weird. They put you in a private room and then give you a public gown.

–Milton Berle

A guy is eating a bald eagle and gets caught by the game warden. He's brought to court for killing an endangered species. The judge says, "Are you aware that eating a bald eagle is a federal offense?"

The guy answers, "Yes, but I have an explanation ... I got lost in the woods and didn't have anything to eat for two weeks. I saw this bald eagle swooping down for fish in a lake. I figured I might be able to steal some fish as the eagle grabbed them. Unfortunately, when I went to grab for the fish, my fist hit the eagle in the head and killed 'im. I reckoned that, since the eagle was dead, I might as well eat it since it would be a waste to just let it rot."

After a brief recess, the judge comes back with his ruling.

"Due to the extreme conditions you endured, added to the fact that the bald eagle's death was accidental rather than intentional, I find you not guilty."

As an aside, the judge asks the guy, "By the way,

what does a bald eagle taste like?

The guy responds, "The best way to describe it is that it tastes like a cross between an owl and an egret."

A crestfallen man comes home from the doctor.

"What's wrong, dear?" asks his wife.

"The doctor informed me that I've only got eight hours to live. I'll tell you what - let's go out for the most expensive dinner in town and then we'll dance 'til dawn."

"Oh, that's great for you," the wife replies. "You don't have to get up in the morning."

> *The second day of a diet is always easier than the first. By the second day you're off it.*
>
> —Jackie Gleason

There's one way to find out if a man is honest — ask him. If he says "yes" you know he's crooked.

–Groucho Marx

Sam and Moe were rocking on a porch in the blistering heat of Miami Beach. Having talked about everything under the sun during their long friendship, Sam was grasping for a new topic of conversation.

"Tell me, Moe, have you read Marx?" Sam asked.

"Yes," replied Moe. "And you know, I think it's these wicker chairs."

A man rushed into the doctor's office and shouted, "Doctor, I think I'm shrinking!"

The doctor calmly responded, "Now, take it easy. You'll just have to be a little patient."

Procrastination Punchlines

Maybe you've heard about the woman who procrastinated about everything. She's the mother of triplets aged seven, eight and nine.

Then there was the case of the procrastinating proctologist who got behind in his work.

Have you heard about the new support group called Procrastinator's Anonymous? Whenever you feel like you're about to put something off, you call another procrastinator and in a couple of weeks they come over to talk.

Book salesman: "This book will do half your work for you."
Procrastinator: "Good. I'll take two!"

There were procrastinators even in Revolutionary War days. In fact, they had their own unit. The were called The Last Minutemen.

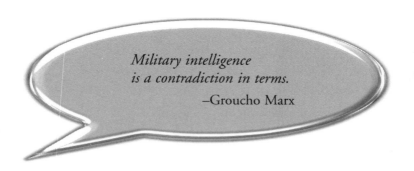

*Military intelligence
is a contradiction in terms.*
–Groucho Marx

> *My friend George walked his dog, all at once. Walked him from Boston to Ft. Lauderdale, and said, "Now you're done."*
>
> –Steven Wright

Benson's new job as a national salesman for a big company promised to have him on the road more often than not. Concerned for his wife's security on those occasions when he'd be away, he decided to stop at a pet shop to look at watchdogs.

When the pet shop owner showed him a French poodle Benson smirked, "C'mon, that dog couldn't hurt a flea."

"Ah, but you don't understand," said the pet shop owner. "This dog knows karate."

With that, the pet shop owner pointed to a two-by-four and commanded, "Karate the wood!"

The little dog split it in half. The pet shop owner then pointed to a thick telephone directory and instructed, "Karate the telephone book!"

Again, the dog split the book in two.

Benson was convinced. He bought the dog and brought it home to his wife, explaining that he'd purchased a watchdog for her.

When she saw the tiny French poodle she scoffed, "That little thing. You've got to be kidding."

Benson remarked, "But this poodle is incredible. He's a karate expert."

"Yeah, right," Benson's wife said. "Karate my foot."

Then there was the crossword puzzle maker who, when he died, was buried six down and three across.

Q: *If a Czar's wife is a Czarina, what would you call their children?*

A: *Czardines.*

My brother-in-law died. He was a karate expert, then joined the army. The first time he saluted, he killed himself.

—Henny Youngman

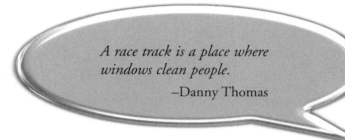

A race track is a place where windows clean people.

—Danny Thomas

Q: *What did the first stoplight say to the second stoplight?*

A: *Don't look - I'm changing!*

After going through six jobs in as

many months, Jim "The Crash" Tomlinson landed a job at a warehouse. One day, while showing off, he lost control of the forklift and drove it through a door and off the loading dock.

Surveying the damage, the owner shook his head and told Jim that he'd have to withhold 10 percent of Jim's wages to pay for the repairs.

"How much will it cost?" asked Jim.

"About $7,500," replied the owner.

"Hooray!" exclaimed Jim. "I've finally got job security!"

Charlie hadn't been feeling well so he went to his doctor for a complete checkup. Afterward, the doctor came out with the results.

"I'm afraid I have some very bad news," the doctor said. "You're dying, and you don't have much time left."

"Oh, that's terrible!" moaned Charlie. "Tell me, Doc. How long have I got left?"

"Ten," the doctor said sadly.

"Ten?" Charlie asked. "Ten what? Months? Weeks? What?"

"Nine..."

I don't like country music, but I don't mean to denigrate those who do. And for the people who like country music, denigrate means "put down."

—Bob Newhart

> *The problem with the designated driver program, it's not a desirable job. But if you ever get sucked into doing it, have fun with it. At the end of the night, drop them off at the wrong house.*
>
> —Jeff Foxworthy

Deep in an African jungle, a guy is

fishing in the river when he hears a rumbling sound behind him. He turns around and finds himself face to face with an 800-pound lion. Immediately, the fisherman lets go of his pole and drops to his knees in desperate prayer. After a few moments, he happens to catch sight of the lion right beside him, on his knees with paws raised in supplication. Surprised, the fisherman says, "Now see here. I am on my knees praying to my Lord for deliverance. You're only a dumb animal. What could you possibly be doing?"

"Whaddaya think, Bud?" says the lion. "I'm saying grace."

The owner of a big law firm, his secretary and a paralegal are walking through a park on their way to lunch when they come upon an antique oil lamp. The owner rubs the lamp and - poof! - a genie appears.

The genie says, "I usually grant three wishes when I'm found, so I'll give each of you just one."

She asks the secretary what she would like first.

"I want to be in the Caribbean, sunning on the beach without a care in the world."

Poof! The secretary disappears.

Then the paralegal is asked what he'd like.

"I want to be in Hawaii with gorgeous girls all around me."

Poof! He's gone.

"And what do you want?" the genie asks the boss.

"I want those two back in the office right after lunch."

My father originated the limbo dance — trying to get into a pay toilet.
—Slappy White

> *Marriage is nature's way of keeping*
> *people from fighting with strangers.*
> —Alan King

"This jigsaw puzzle is driving me crazy," said Hubert to his friend on the phone.

"What's so difficult about it?" asked his buddy.

"Well, for one, there are so many pieces. They're all the same color and the edges aren't flat - they're crinkly."

"What's the picture on the box?" his buddy inquired.

"A big rooster," Hubert replied.

"Okay Hubie, now listen very carefully. Pick up all the pieces and put the corn flakes back in the box."

An Arkansas State trooper pulled over a speeding pickup truck on I-40. He said to the driver, "Got any ID?"

The toothless driver grinned and said, "'Bout what?"

Q: *Why was the employee fired from the orange juice factory?*

A: *He couldn't concentrate.*

A vacationer was cruising just off the coast of Florida when his boat suddenly capsized. Fearful of alligators, he clung to the boat rather than swim to the shore for safety. He noticed someone standing along the shore and yelled, "Hey, mister, are there any gators in this water?"

The guy shouted back, "No, they haven't been in these waters for years."

The vacationer, pacified by the comment, began swimming toward shore.

With a considerable distance left to swim, he hollered, "How come there are no gators?"

"The sharks got 'em."

The average dog is a nicer person than the average person.

–Andy Rooney

Human beings are the only creatures that allow their children to come back home.
–Bill Cosby

Little Stevie was a Jewish boy

who lived in a small town in Italy where the only school was a parochial one. He came home one day and complained to his mother that the nuns were always asking Catholic questions and he could never answer them.

"I tell you what, Stevie," said his mother. "I'm going to write down answers on the inside of your shirt. That way you'll be prepared if a nun calls on you."

Sure enough, the next day Sister Anna asked Stevie who he thought was the most famous woman in the New Testament.

Stevie looked down inside his shirt, then looked up and said, "Why, Mary, of course."

"And who was her husband?" asked Sister Anna.

"Joseph," replied Stevie.

"Excellent," remarked Sister Anna. "One final question - What was the name of their son?"

Stevie looked down inside his shirt one more time, then responded, "Tommy Hilfiger."

Off The Wall

Graffiti found on bathoom walls around the world.

Hypochondria is the only disease I haven't got.

Joan of Arc was Noah's wife.

Celibacy is not hereditary.

Betsy Ross was a sew & sew.

Where there's a will there's a delay.

Obesity is widespread.

Weightlifters are biceptual.

John Doe is a nobody.

Jack and Jill are over the hill.

A bird in hand is safer than one overhead.

Insanity is hereditary; you can get it from your children.
—Sam Levenson

Your high school reunion. You get that letter in the mail. You feel like you only have six months to make something of yourself.

–Drew Carey

Two old geezers were playing the sixth hole of a golf course. One of them was on the fairway while the other was searching in the rough. The foursome behind them was growing impatient. Finally, one of the four yelled to the old-timer on the fairway, "Hey, why don't you help your friend find his ball?"

The old guy shouted back, "He's got his ball. He's looking for his club."

Then there was the guy with a B.A., an M.A., and a PhD. The only thing he didn't have was a JOB.